Sets of
Picture Cards

The children in Room 3
have lots of picture cards.

They have cards about horses,
and trucks, and dinosaurs,
and many other things.

Today the children are staying inside
because it is raining.
They are swapping their cards
to make sets of ten.

"I have nine horse cards,"
said Sarah.
"I need one more
to make my set of ten."

"I have more horse cards than you,"
said Max. "I have twelve.
I can give you one of mine."

12 > 9

Max gave Sarah the card
that she needed.

"Now I have ten cards
with pictures of horses," said Sarah.
"I have a set."

Sarah's horse cards
$$9 + 1 = 10$$

Max's horse cards
$$12 - 1 = 11$$

Who has the most horse cards now —
Max or Sarah?

Max still has more horse cards than Sarah, because 11 is greater than 10.

11 > 10

Max likes dinosaurs.
He wants to make
a set of dinosaur cards.
He has five and he needs five more.

Sarah has **thirteen** dinosaur cards,
but she wants to keep a set for herself.

How many cards does Sarah give to Max?

Sarah gives Max **three** cards,
because thirteen take away three leaves ten.

13 − 3 = 10

Now Max has eight dinosaur cards.
He had five
and Sarah gave him three more.

$$5 + 3 = 8$$

But eight is less than ten.

$$8 < 10$$

How many more dinosaur cards
does Max need to make his set of ten?

Max needs two more cards,
because **eight** and **two** make **ten**.

8 + 2 = 10

Sarah has truck cards and cat cards.
She wants to make a set of cards
with pictures of cats.
She only has six of these cards.
Six is less than ten.

$$6 < 10$$

How many more does she need
to make ten?

Sarah needs **four** more cards, because six and four make ten.

Max looked at all of his cards,
and he looked at Sarah's cards.

"I will swap you these four cat cards
for those six truck cards," he said.

"Yes," laughed Sarah.
"Then I will have a set of cat cards,
because six and four make ten."

$$6 + 4 = 10$$

"And I will have a set of truck cards,"
said Max,
"because four and six make ten."

$$4 + 6 = 10$$

Did you know?

Six and four is the same as four and six.

$$6 + 4 = 4 + 6$$

Twelve is **greater** than **nine**.

$$12 > 9$$

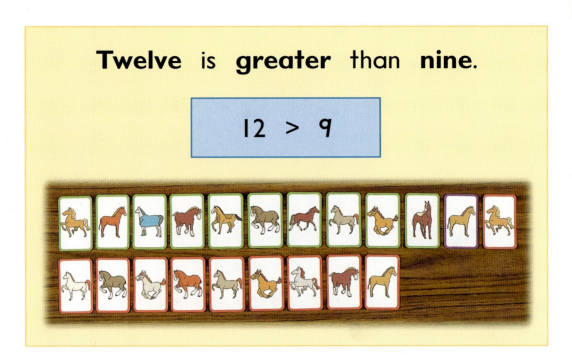

Eight is **less** than **ten**.

$$8 < 10$$

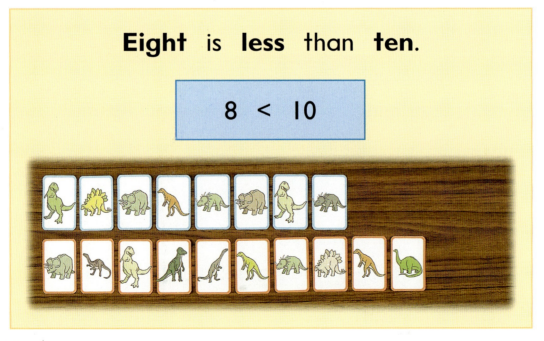